BEADING ON TIGER TAIL

Beading wire (also called tiger tail) is used for stringing beads and findings to make durable, flexible jewellery. Previously, stringing was done on thread, but the ease of use, durability and flexibility of tiger tail have made it one of the most widely used materials for stringing beads today.

Tiger tail is made up of multiple strands of fine stainless steel wire, twisted together and covered with a nylon coating. It is available in different colours, diameters and break strengths: the most commonly used is seven-strand wire, but up to forty-nine-strand wire is also available. Surprisingly, the more strands the tiger tail is made up of, the more flexible and fluid the wire.

Tips for use

- Unless you are 'floating' beads on the wire (see page 56), ensure that all gaps between beads are closed up so that no wire shows.
- Don't pull or stretch the wire too tight before crimping (see page 14) or the movement of the necklace will be stiff.
- It can be hard to remove or replace a flattened crimp bead without damaging the beading wire. Always use a new crimp bead, even if you have successfully removed a flattened bead, to ensure the security of the crimp and the durability and strength of your wire.
- One way to ensure your necklace is the desired length is to place one end of the clasp at the middle of the back of the neck and see where the beads fall in the front. You can then add or remove beads as required.

TOOLS

| Chain-nose pliers | Bent-nose pliers | Round-nose pliers | Flush cutters | Bradawl |

DINNER DATE NECKLACE

Creamy pearls framed with square diamante spacers surrounded by jet faceted crystal rondelles make up this exquisitely classic necklace of understated elegance. Just like a 'little black dress', this quick and easy-to-make ensemble is the perfect accessory to any woman's wardrobe.

What you learn

✎ How to use wire guardians to protect and finish the clasp ends of the jewellery piece
✎ How to use crimp beads
✎ How to open and close a jump ring
✎ How to attach a clasp to a jewellery piece

MATERIALS
1 14mm ivory pearl
64 8 x 6mm faceted jet crystal rondelles
2 3mm round silver-coloured metal beads
2 8mm square diamante spacer
1 silver-coloured toggle clasp
2 silver-coloured wire guardians
2 2mm silver-coloured crimp beads
2 6mm silver-coloured jump rings
60–70cm [23½–27½in] silver seven-strand beading wire/tiger tail

Crimp beads

Crimps, or crimp beads, are small beads or tubes made of soft metal that hold when flattened. They are used for attaching clasps or beads to beading wire as well as for floating beads on wire, thread or certain chains. Crimp beads come in different sizes and metal finishes.

The square shape of the diamante spacers is mirrored in this antiqued decorative silver-plated toggle clasp.

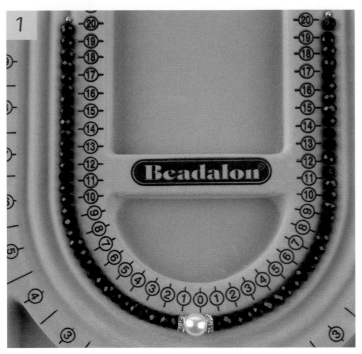

1 Lay out the design of the necklace on a beading board or mat, starting at the top of one side and working around and back to the other side as follows:
- round silver metal bead
- 32 jet crystal rondelles
- square diamante spacer
- pearl
- square diamante spacer
- 32 jet crystal rondelles
- round silver metal bead

Thread one end of the beading wire/tiger tail through a crimp bead and around a wire guardian following the instructions below. This process is referred to later in the book as 'crimping'.

THREADING WIRE THROUGH A CRIMP BEAD AND WIRE GUARDIAN

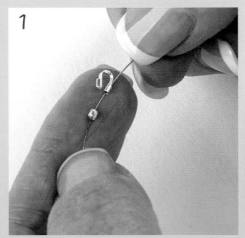

1 Thread about 3cm (1½in) of one end of the beading wire/tiger tail through a crimp bead and around a wire guardian.

2 Pass the short end of the beading wire/tiger tail back through the crimp bead.

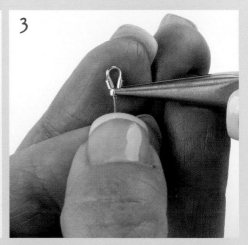

3 Pull the wire tight with the crimp bead across the base of the wire guardian. With chain-nose pliers, flatten the crimp bead.

2

2 Starting with a silver metal bead at one end of the beads laid out in step 1, string beads onto the beading wire/tiger tail, ensuring that they pass over both the short and long tails of beading wire.

3 Pass the beading wire/tiger tail through a second crimp bead and around a wire guardian.

4 Pass the beading wire/tiger tail back through the crimp bead, the silver metal bead and two crystal rondelles.

5 Pull the wire tight to eliminate any gaps or exposed wire. With chain-nose pliers, flatten the crimp bead across the base of the wire guardian. Trim away any excess beading wire using flush cutters.

3

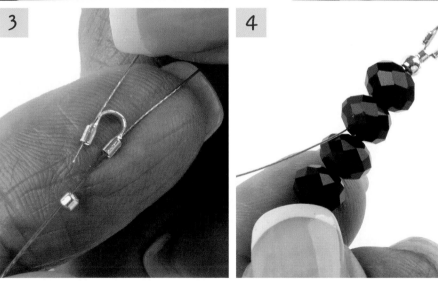

4

5

6 Use chain-nose pliers to open a small jump ring – see 'Opening and Closing a Jump Ring', below. Slip one side of the clasp onto the jump ring and attach to one end of the necklace and close with the pliers.

7 Repeat step 6 at the other end of the necklace.

OPENING AND CLOSING A JUMP RING

1 Grasp each side of the join in the jump ring using two pairs of pliers (I prefer to use one pair of bent-nose pliers and one pair of chain-nose pliers).

2 To open the jump ring, carefully twist it apart with the two pairs of pliers – do not pull the ring apart.

3 To close the jump ring, twist the ends back together so they go slightly past each other, then bring them back in line. The ends will usually click into place and you can feel them rub together for a perfect fit.

Design Inspiration

Handmade ceramic tube beads add interest and make an attractive focus to this classy necklace. Faceted crystals in the same muted green, separated by jet crystal bicones, add sparkle to the matt finish of the glazed tube beads.

TROPICAL LAGOON
NECKLACE

This stylish, longer-length necklace with matching bracelet is created using beautiful sparkling faceted rondelles and crystal bicones in shades of blue touched with a hint of lilac.

MATERIALS

16 12 x 10mm sapphire crystal rondelles
8 10 x 8mm aqua crystal rondelles
7 10 x 8mm lilac crystal rondelles
32 6mm dark sapphire crystal bicones
32 6mm light aqua crystal bicones
16 6mm teal crystal bicones
14 6mm lilac crystal bicones
16 11/0 satin silver seed beads
1 22mm silver-coloured lobster/trigger clasp
1 8mm silver-coloured jump ring
2 silver-coloured wire guardians
2 2mm silver-coloured crimp beads
1.5m (59in) silver seven-strand beading wire/tiger tail

Creating a matching bracelet couldn't be easier: the technique is exactly the same, with the only difference being the length!

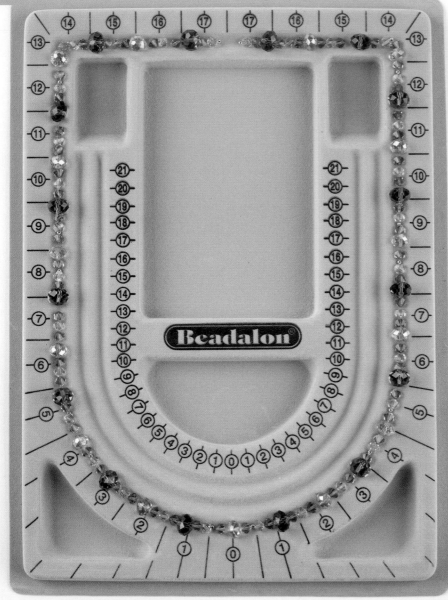

1 Lay out the design of the necklace on a beading board or mat, starting at the top of one side and working around and back to the other side. Start with a silver seed bead, then repeat the following pattern seven times:

- silver seed bead
- light aqua bicone
- dark sapphire bicone
- dark sapphire rondelle
- dark sapphire bicone
- light aqua bicone
- teal bicone
- aqua rondelle
- teal bicone
- light aqua bicone
- dark sapphire bicone
- dark sapphire rondelle
- dark sapphire bicone
- light aqua bicone
- silver seed bead
- lilac bicone
- lilac rondelle
- lilac bicone

Finish the pattern with the following sequence:

- silver seed bead
- light aqua bicone
- dark sapphire bicone
- dark sapphire rondelle
- dark sapphire bicone
- light aqua bicone
- teal bicone
- aqua rondelle
- teal bicone
- light sapphire bicone
- dark sapphire bicone
- dark sapphire rondelle
- dark sapphire bicone
- light sapphire bicone
- silver seed bead

Set the beads aside until step 3.

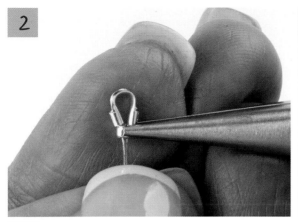

2 Thread about 3cm (1¼in) of one end of the beading wire/tiger tail through a crimp bead and around a wire guardian (see page 12). Pass the short end of the beading wire/tiger tail back through the crimp bead. Pull the wire tight with the crimp bead across the base of the wire guardian. With chain-nose pliers, flatten the crimp bead.

3 String beads onto the beading wire/tiger tail as laid out on the beading board or mat, starting with the silver seed bead at one end and working around to the silver seed bead at the other end.

4 Pass the beading wire/tiger tail through a second crimp bead and around a wire guardian. Pass the beading wire/tiger tail back through the crimp bead, the silver seed bead and the next two beads. Pull the wire tight to eliminate any gaps or exposed wire.

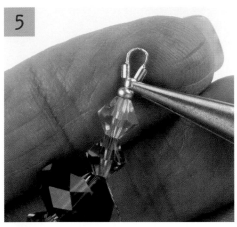

5 With chain-nose pliers, flatten the crimp bead across the base of the wire guardian. Trim away any excess beading wire using flush cutters.

6 Use chain-nose pliers to open a small jump ring. (See 'Opening and Closing a Jump Ring' on page 14.) Slip the lobster/trigger clasp onto the jump ring, attach to one end of the necklace and close.

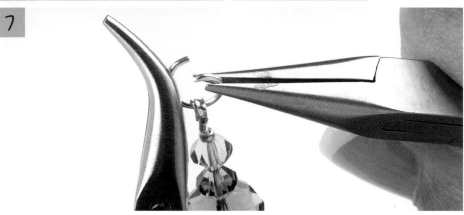

7 Attach an 8mm jump ring to the other end of the necklace to complete the design.

Tips

- Ensure the flattened crimp bead holds both strands of wire. You can check this by pulling and wiggling the wire guardian above the crimp.
- For additional security, you can add a second crimp bead above the first one or use a crimp tube.
- When starting to thread beads, ensure that they also pass over the short tail end both to hide it and give a secure, neat finish.

Design Inspiration

A repeating pattern of creamy pearls and silver beads is used to create this lovely long-length necklace. The mix of different shapes and sizes, from freshwater pearl chips and sticks to silver cubes, shiny silver rounds and sparkling pavé rondelles, combine to offer a stylish appeal.

AUTUMN ACORNS NECKLACE

MATERIALS

38 12 x 10mm amethyst crystal rondelles
4 10mm bayong wood beads
4 10mm palm wood beads
10 8mm robles wood beads
30 9 x 2mm wood disc beads
10 8mm gunmetal bead
10 10 x 12mm antiqued silver double floral bead caps
1 antiqued silver-coloured leaf toggle clasp
2 silver-coloured wire guardians
2 2mm silver-coloured crimp beads
1.5m (59in) silver seven-strand beading wire/tiger tail

Why should beautiful clasps be hidden at the back of the neck or under hair? Here, we have combined a variety of natural wood beads to provide interest and texture between antiqued bead caps that blend with the gorgeous leaf-shaped toggle clasp, which is designed to be worn to the side.

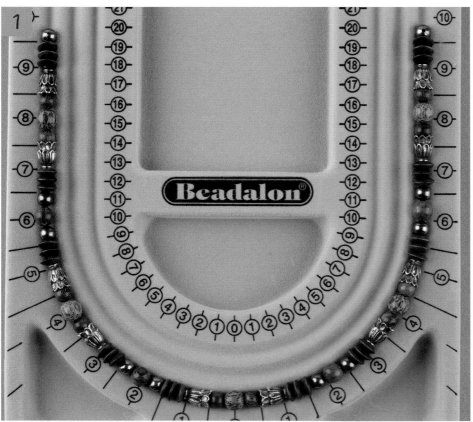

1 Lay out the design of the necklace on a beading board or mat, starting at the top of one side and working around and back to the other side. Repeat the following pattern four times:
• gunmetal bead
• 3 wood disc beads
• bell cap
• 8mm wood bead
• 10mm palm bead (with stripes and dots)
• 8mm wood bead
• bell cap
• 3 wood disc beads
• gunmetal bead
• 10mm bayong bead

Finish the pattern with the following sequence:
• gunmetal bead
• 3 wood disc beads
• bell cap
• 8mm wood bead
• 10mm palm bead (with stripes and dots)
• 8mm wood bead
• bell cap
• 3 wood disc beads
• gunmetal bead

2 Following the instructions on page 12, thread about 3cm (1¼in) of one end of the beading wire/tiger tail through a crimp bead, around a wire guardian and back through the crimp bead before securing the crimp by flattening it with chain-nose pliers across the base of the wire guardian. String beads onto the beading wire/tiger tail as laid out on the beading board, starting with the gunmetal bead at one end and working around to the gunmetal bead at the other end. Pass the beading wire/tiger tail through a crimp bead and around a wire guardian. Pass the beading wire/tiger tail back through the crimp bead, the gunmetal bead and the three disc beads.

3 Pull the wire tight to eliminate any gaps or exposed wire. With chain-nose pliers, flatten the crimp bead across the base of the wire guardian. Trim away any excess beading wire using flush cutters.

4 Use chain-nose pliers to open a small jump ring. (See 'Opening and Closing a Jump Ring' on page 14.) Slip one side of the clasp onto the jump ring and attach to one end of the necklace and close.

5 Finally, repeat step 4 with the other side of the clasp.

Design Inspiration

The clasp can also be worn as the focal point of the necklace, especially when it is as beautiful as this decorative toggle clasp! The floral clasp perfectly enhances this exquisite strand of pale pink faceted rondelles, which are embellished with creamy freshwater pearls and sparkling diamante spacers.

LOVER'S DREAM NECKLACE

MATERIALS

112 6–8mm ivory round freshwater pearls

2 10mm white crystal glitter balls/beads

1 10mm red glitter ball/bead

5 3mm round silver-coloured metal beads

1 silver-coloured heart lobster/trigger clasp, 28 x 12mm (1 x ½in)

1 8mm silver-coloured jump ring

2 silver-coloured wire guardians

2 2mm silver-coloured crimp beads

2.5m (98½in) silver seven-strand beading wire/tiger tail

1 9mm white satin tassel

10–15cm (4–6in) 24-gauge silver-coloured wire

A silky tassel below sparkling glitter balls is the eye-catching focus of this longer-length necklace of rich, creamy freshwater pearls.

What you learn

✎ How to prepare a tassel

✎ How to make a wrapped loop

PREPARING THE TASSEL

1 If there is a loop above the tassel, remove it, using flush cutters.

Lobster clasps (also called trigger clasps or parrot clasps) can come in many different shapes and sizes, and can be made from different materials. This antiqued, silver-plated clasp with its heart decoration was chosen specially to reflect the 'Lover's Dream' theme!

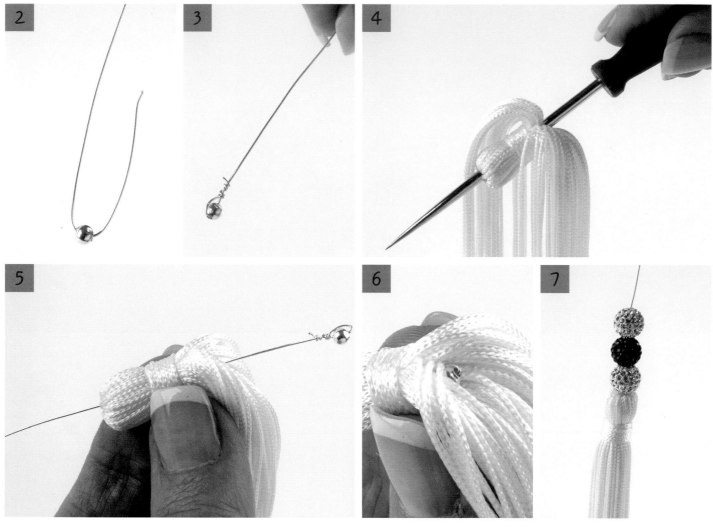

2 Thread a silver metal bead 3cm (1¼in) from one end of the silver wire.

3 Wrap the 3cm (1¼in) of wire around the other end of the silver bead. This does not have to be a precise or neat wrap.

4 Turn the tassel upside-down so that the threads fall to the side. Poke the bradawl from the centre of the upside-down tassel down through the head of the tassel to the top end. Twist the bradawl to make a channel.

5 Pass the end of the wire end through the channel formed by the bradawl in step 4 and pull it through...

6 ...until the bead lodges at the base of the tassel head.

7 Turn the tassel upright so that the bead is hidden by the fringe and a length of wire extends through the centre of the tassel head. String the three glitter balls onto the wire then make a wrapped loop above the beads (see opposite page).

HOW TO MAKE A WRAPPED LOOP

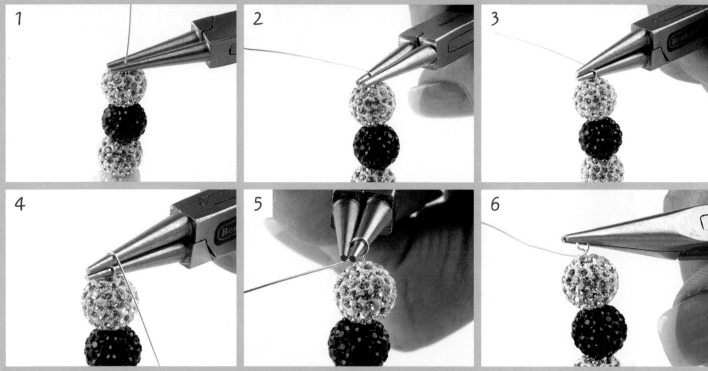

The finished loop.

1 Using round-nose pliers, hold the wire tight against the bead.

2 With your finger, bend the wire at a right angle to the round-nose pliers. The pliers should be horizontal, as shown above.

3 Shift the barrels of the round-nose pliers so they are vertical.

4 Use your fingers to pull the wire tight around the top barrel of the pliers, then down. Pull so that the wire is tight around the barrel and down as far as it can go.

5 Shift the barrels again to make them horizontal. Use your fingers to pull the wire around the barrel of the pliers to form a complete loop.

6 Twist the wire two to three times, or as many as required, around the gap between the topmost glitter ball and the loop. Use flush cutters to trim the end of the wire.

CREATING THE NECKLACE

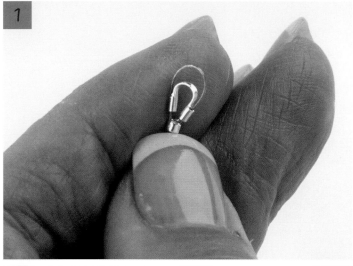

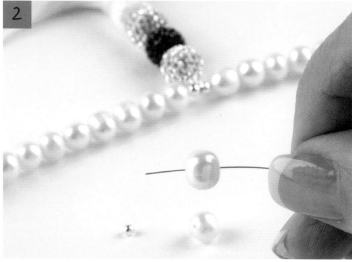

Tips

- At step 3, sometimes the holes in the pearls are too small to take two strands of beading wire. If that is the case, it is sufficient to pass the wire through the metal bead only.
- Ensure that the flattened crimp bead holds both strands of wire. You can check this by pulling and wiggling on the clasp above the crimp.
- For additional security, you can add a second crimp bead above the first one or use a crimp tube.

1 Thread about 3cm (1½in) of one end of the beading wire/tiger tail through a crimp bead and around a wire guardian. Pass the short end of the beading wire/tiger tail back through the crimp bead. Pull the wire tight with the crimp bead across the base of the wire guardian. With chain-nose pliers, flatten the crimp bead. See page 12 for the full instructions.

2 String onto the other end of the beading wire a small silver metal bead, half of the pearls and a second small silver metal bead. Continue by adding the tassel, a third silver metal bead, the other half of the pearls and a fourth silver metal bead.

3 Pass the beading wire/tiger tail through a second crimp bead and around a wire guardian. Then pass the beading wire/tiger tail back through the crimp bead and the silver metal bead and one or two pearls. Pull the wire tight to eliminate any gaps or exposed wire. With chain-nose pliers, flatten the crimp bead across the base of the wire guardian. Trim away any excess beading wire using flush cutters.

4 Use chain-nose pliers to open a small jump ring. (See 'Opening and Closing a Jump Ring' on page 14.) Slip one side of the clasp onto the jump ring and attach to one end of the necklace and close. Attach the 8mm jump ring to the other end of the necklace.

Design Inspiration

Why not try a different coloured tassel or even a pendant? Be inspired by this stunning Swarovski crystal, and this heirloom turquoise heart pendant given to me by my favourite aunt. The necklace can reflect and enhance the pendant, as can be seen with the irregular shape of the jasper and the polished smooth surface of the round turquoise beads that add an interesting contrast reflected in the heart pendant.

Wildfire is a braided thread with a smooth, thermally-bonded coating that gives it strength and durability. It is strong, waterproof and has limited stretch. It cannot be pierced with a needle and the ends will not fray, making it easy to thread through needles. It is colourfast, knottable and very supple.

Wildfire comes in 0.15mm or 0.20mm diameter. Until very recently, it was available only in a colour choice of black or frost (white); however, new colours are beginning to come onto the market – notably green, red and blue.

Tips for use

• The stiffness of Wildfire means that you don't have to use a needle but a split eye needle can make it easier and quicker to string beads onto the thread.

• After making an overhand knot with one or more threads, use chain-nose pliers to pull each short tail above the knot individually. This will pull out any slack and make it a small tight knot.

About calottes or bead tips

Calottes, or bead tips, are designed to conceal and protect knots as well as to create a secure connection to jump rings and clasps. Bead tips complete jewellery designs with a clean and professional finish as they look like small, metal beads at each end of a strand of thread. Calottes are available in a variety of precious and plated metals, fashion finishes and designer styles.

TOOLS

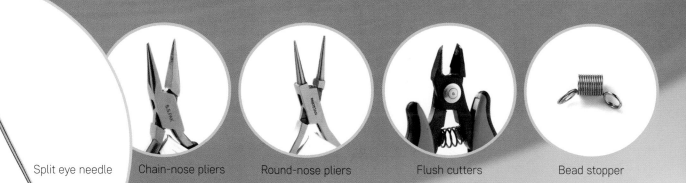

Split eye needle   Chain-nose pliers   Round-nose pliers   Flush cutters   Bead stopper

ALL ABOUT PEARLS BRACELET

The beauty of freshwater pearls is demonstrated perfectly in this gorgeous bracelet where a variety of shapes and sizes creates a lush rope of pearl perfection. The decorative hook clasp and coin pearl charm make every aspect of this piece 'all about pearls'!

What you learn

- How to use bead tips/calottes
- The versatility of thermally-bonded threads
- How to use a bead stopper
- How to make multi-stranded jewellery
- How to use charms to enhance jewellery pieces

MATERIALS

28 6–8mm round ivory freshwater pearls
42 5–6mm round ivory freshwater pearls
49 4 x 6mm button ivory freshwater pearls
41 4–5mm rice ivory freshwater pearls
9 2.4mm round silver-plated metal beads
2 silver-plated bead tips/calottes
2 2mm silver-plated crimp beads
3 6mm silver-plated jump rings
1 silver ball-end headpin
1 antiqued silver-plated decorative clasp
1 15 x 12mm coin-shaped freshwater pearl
1.5m (59in) frost Wildfire beading thread
Clear nail varnish or clear drying adhesive

Use clear nail varnish to seal the knots made in the Wildfire thread.

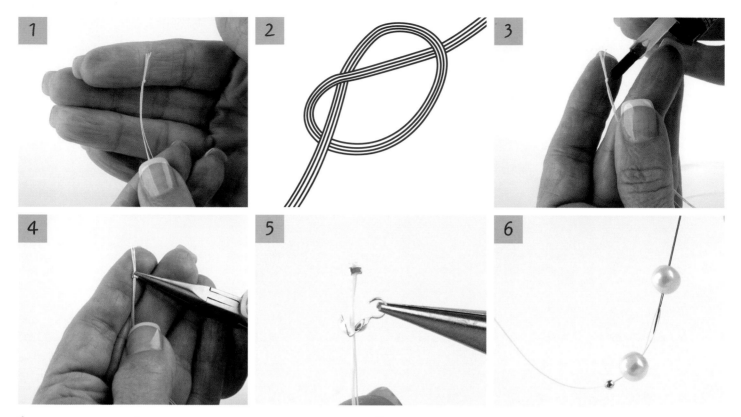

1 Cut the Wildfire into four equal lengths – about 30–35cm (11¾–13¾in) long.

2 Tie the four lengths together in an overhand knot (the way you would tie a balloon) about 2.5cm (1in) from one end. Pull the knot tight.

3 Seal the knot with clear nail varnish and allow to dry.

4 Pass the short ends of all four strands of Wildfire through a crimp bead and slip the crimp bead over the knot. With chain-nose pliers, flatten the crimp bead. Trim away the excess Wildfire from above the flattened crimp bead using flush cutters.

5 Pass the four strands of Wildfire through a bead tip/calotte, going from the inside to the outside of the cup, allowing the flattened crimp to rest inside the bead tip/calotte. With chain-nose pliers, gently close the cup of the bead tip/calotte over the flattened crimp.

6 Thread a split eye needle with approximately 3cm (1¼in) of one strand of the threads. String on a small silver metal bead then the large round (6–8mm) pearls. Finish the strand with a second small silver metal bead.

USING A BEAD STOPPER

Bead stoppers are useful in securing the end of a project in process so that the beads don't fall off! Some bead stoppers are available with plastic covering the wire loops for ease and comfort. To attach a bead stopper:

1 Pinch the wire loops at either side of the wire coil, which will open up space between the coils.

2 Pass the tiger tail (beading wire) or thread into the space between two coils.

3 Release the wire loops at either side of the wire coil, ensuring that the tiger tail or thread is caught securely between the coils.

Note: Multiple strands can be held by one bead stopper if desired.

7 Remove the needle and keep the pearls from coming off with a bead stopper.

8 Repeat steps 6 and 7 with the medium round (5–6mm) pearls, then the small button-shaped pearls and finally the very small rice-shaped pearls, each on a strand of Wildfire. Ensure that all the strands of pearls are the same length. Pass all four threads through a second bead tip/calotte, this time from the outside to the inside of the cup.

9 With two strands in one hand and two strands in the other hand, tie a reef (square) knot – left over right, pull tight, then right over left and pull tight. Be sure the beads are tight against the bead tip/calotte, without any gaps of thread showing below, but not so tight that the strands are stiff. Pull the strands tight to make the knot as small as possible. Repeat, then seal the double knot with clear nail varnish and allow to dry.

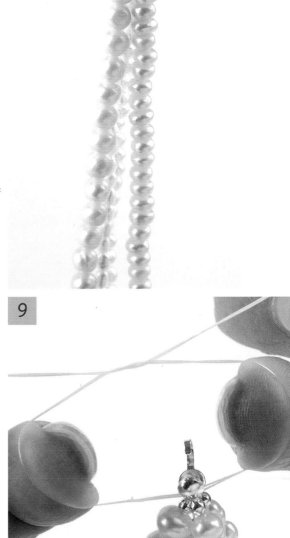

10 Pass the four strands of thread through a crimp bead and slip the crimp bead over the knot. With chain-nose pliers, flatten the crimp bead. Trim away excess thread from above the flattened crimp bead. Gently close the cup of the bead tip/calotte over the flattened crimp bead with the chain-nose pliers.

11 With round-nose pliers, close the hook above the bead tip/calotte to form a loop.

12 Use chain-nose pliers to open a small jump ring. (See 'Opening and Closing a Jump Ring' on page 14.) Slip one side of the clasp onto the jump ring and attach to one end of the bracelet and close. Repeat with the other end of the bracelet.

13 Make a coin pearl charm by threading the pearl onto a ball end headpin followed by a small silver metal bead. Form a wrapped loop (see page 29) above the metal bead.

14 Use chain-nose pliers to open a small jump ring. Attach the charms to the jump ring that is used to fix one side of the clasp to one end of the bracelet.

Tips

• The holes in freshwater pearls can be very small and can vary from bead to bead on the same strand. You may have to be persistent in pulling the needle through smaller holes. Using chain-nose pliers to pull the needle can help (but be prepared to bend your needle). Allow for extra pearls, and be selective about which you use. Alternatively, use a pearl reamer or bradawl to enlarge the holes of pearls.

• Pearls may shift over time and a tiny bit of thread may show between beads. A thermally-bonded thread like Wildfire is ideal for threading pearls: it has almost no stretch, and the frost colour will blend in with the pearls.

• Clear nail varnish not only seals knots and dries clear, but the brush also makes it easy to ensure that every angle of the knot is coated.

• Using chain-nose pliers to pull each individual short strand of thread above a knot will help tighten the knot and make it as small as it can be.

• To cut thermally-bonded thread, I prefer to use sharp flush cutters as they allow me to get close to the crimp bead and don't require any tension on the strands above the knot.

• To wear this bracelet as a twisted rope, twist the strands before attaching the clasp.

Design inspiration

The mixed textures of natural turquoise chips, freshwater pearls and smooth, round coral beads are twisted in and out to create this eye-catching bracelet with antiqued elephant charms.

QUEEN OF SHEBA NECKLACE

Sparkling black crystals wind their way between subtle tones of gold and bronze seed beads to create this classic necklace, fit for the Queen of Sheba. It can be worn as a multi-stranded necklace or twisted into a rope for a more tailored look. Either way, it is elegant and eye-catching!

MATERIALS
290–300 11/0 bronze seed beads
290–300 11/0 black seed beads
200–220 8/0 gold metallic seed beads
200–220 8/0 copper metallic seed beads
175 3 x 4mm jet crystal rondelles
3m (118in) black Wildfire beading thread
2 gold-coloured bead tips/calottes
2 2mm gold-coloured crimp beads
4 5mm gold-coloured jump rings
1 antiqued gold-coloured toggle clasp
Clear nail varnish or clear drying adhesive

1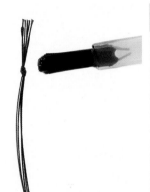

2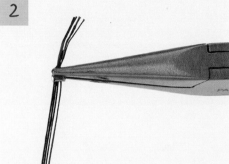

3

1 Cut the Wildfire into five equal lengths, each about 60cm (23½in) long. Tie the five lengths together in an overhand knot about 2.5cm (1in) from one end. Pull the knot tight, and seal it with clear nail varnish. Allow to dry.

2 Pass the short ends of all five strands of Wildfire through a crimp bead and slip the crimp bead over the knot. With chain-nose pliers, flatten the crimp bead. Then trim away any excess Wildfire from above the flattened crimp bead using flush cutters.

3 Pass the five strands of Wildfire through a bead tip/calotte, going from the inside to the outside of the cup. Gently close the cup of the bead tip/calotte over the flattened crimp with chain-nose pliers.

The clasp, opposite left
The antiqued, gold-plated toggle clasp blends nicely with the twisted strands of gold and bronze elements in this elegant necklace.

4 Thread a split eye needle with approximately 3cm (1¼in) of one strand of the threads. String on enough bronze seed beads for your chosen length of necklace. Remove the needle and keep the beads in place with a bead stopper (see page 37).

5 Repeat step 4 with the black seed beads, the gold metallic seed beads, the copper metallic seed beads, black seed beads, satin gold seed beads and then the jet crystal rondelles, each on their own strand of Wildfire. Ensure all strands of beads are the same length.

6 Pass all five threads through a second bead tip/calotte, this time from the outside to the inside of the cup.

7 With two strands in one hand and three in the other hand, tie a reef (square) knot, as shown (see also page 37). Make sure the beads are tight against the bead tip/calotte, without any gaps of thread showing below, but not so tight that the strands are stiff. Pull the knot tight to make it as small as possible and seal it with clear nail varnish. Allow to dry.

8 Pass the five strands of thread through a crimp bead and slip the crimp bead over the knot. With chain-nose pliers, flatten the crimp bead. Trim away excess thread from above the flattened crimp bead.

9 With chain-nose pliers, gently close the cup of the bead tip/calotte over the flattened crimp.

10 With round-nose pliers, close the hook above the bead tip/calotte to form a loop. Use chain-nose pliers to open a small jump ring. (See 'Opening and Closing a Jump Ring' on page 14.) Slip one side of the clasp onto the jump ring and attach to one end of the necklace and close. Repeat with the other side of the clasp on the other end of the necklace.

Design inspiration

The richness of creamy freshwater pearls beside sparkling faceted crystals with an Aurora Borealis finish is twisted with satin rocailles and matt black seed beads to create an elegant rope of gorgeous beads.

CONFETTI NECKLACE

Sparkling faceted crystals and creamy glass pearls are interspersed among silvery satin seed beads giving an illusion of bits of confetti floating on the necklace.

What you learn

✎ How to mix beads of different sizes to create an illusion of floating confetti

MATERIALS

950–1000 10/0 satin silver seed beads
19 4mm white glass pearls
6 10mm white glass pearls
6 6 x 4mm faceted AB crystal rondelles
5 8 x 6mm faceted AB crystal rondelles
2m (78¾in) frost Wildfire beading thread
2 silver-coloured calotte/bead tips
2 2mm silver-coloured crimp beads
2 5mm silver-coloured jump rings
1 silver-coloured toggle clasp
Clear nail varnish or clear drying adhesive

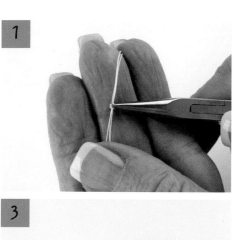

1 Cut the Wildfire into three equal lengths, each about 60cm (23½in). Tie the three lengths together in an overhand knot (see page 36) about 2.5cm (1in) from one end. Pull the knot tight, then seal it with clear nail varnish. Allow to dry. Pass the short ends of all three strands of Wildfire through a crimp bead and slip the crimp bead over the knot. With chain-nose pliers, flatten the crimp bead.

2 Trim away excess Wildfire from above the flattened crimp bead. Pass the three strands of Wildfire through a bead tip/calotte, going from the inside to the outside of the cup.

3 With chain-nose pliers, gently close the cup of the bead tip/calotte over the flattened crimp.

4 Thread a split eye needle with approximately 3cm (1¼in) of one strand of the threads.

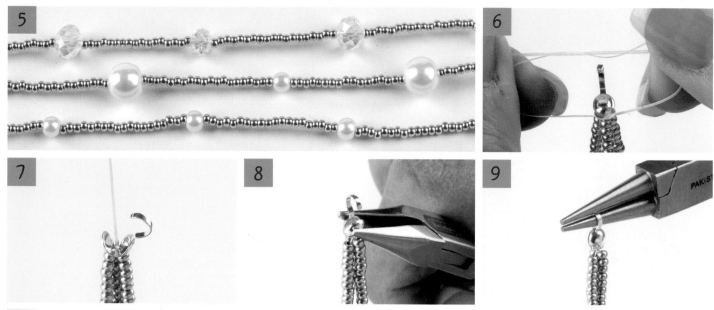

5 Fill the first strand with silver seed beads and AB crystal rondelles, with approximately 2.5–3cm (1–1¼in) of seed beads between the staggered small and large crystal rondelles.

Fill the second strand with silver seed beads and large and small white pearls with approximately 2.5–3cm (1–1¼in) of seed beads between the pearls. The large and small pearls should be alternated, and should be staggered so that when this strand is laid next to the first strand, the pearls fall between where the crystals are placed, not side-by-side.

Finally, fill the third strand with silver seed beads and small pearls with approximately 2.5–3cm (1–1¼in) of seed beads between the pearls. Stagger the pearls so that when this strand is laid next to the previous two strands, the small pearls fall between where the crystals and alternated pearls are placed, not side-by-side.

6 Pass all three threads through a second bead tip/calotte, this time from the outside to the inside of the cup. With two strands in one hand and one strand in the other hand, tie a reef (square) knot (see page 37). Be sure that the beads are tight against the bead tip/calotte, without gaps of thread showing below, but not so tight that the strands are stiff. Make the knot as small as possible, then seal it with clear nail varnish and allow it to dry.

7 Pass the three strands of thread through a crimp bead and slip the crimp bead over the knot. With chain-nose pliers, flatten the crimp bead. Trim away excess thread from above the flattened crimp bead.

8 With chain-nose pliers, gently close the cup of the calotte over the flattened crimp.

9 With round-nose pliers, close the hook above the calotte to form a loop.

10 Use chain-nose pliers to open a small jump ring. (See 'Opening and Closing a Jump Ring' on page 14.) Slip one side of the clasp onto the jump ring and attach to one end of the necklace and close. Repeat to attach the T-bar to the other end of the necklace.

Tip

• To wear this necklace as a twisted rope, twist the strands before attaching the clasp at step 10.

Design inspiration

Exquisite Czech crystal bicones of coordinating colours and different sizes are the confetti in this stunning eye-catching necklace of twenty-four strands of assorted seed beads in chocolate, copper, amber and beige.

TROPICAL RAINFOREST NECKLACE

Elegantly long, this lariat-style necklace features an assortment of seed beads in shades of green with shiny silver accents. A beaded fringe dangles below a stylish knot to add texture and interest to this fabulous piece.

Typically a lariat necklace is a long necklace without a clasp at the back, and fastened with a knot at the front. However, I have designed this particular piece with a clasp, so it is not necessary for the wearer to tie a knot in the strands of seed beads every time the necklace is worn.

What you learn

- ✎ How to make a lariat–style necklace
- ✎ How to create a beaded fringe

MATERIALS

2,500–2,600 11/0 seed beads (assorted green and silver shades)

12 6/0 silver seed beads

4 4mm green crystal bicones

3 6mm green crystal bicones

2 4mm AB crystal bicones

4 6mm AB crystal bicones

4m (157½in) frost Wildfire beading thread

2 silver-coloured bead tips/calottes

8 2mm silver-coloured crimp beads

2 6mm silver-coloured jump rings

1 silver-coloured toggle clasp

Clear nail varnish or clear drying adhesive

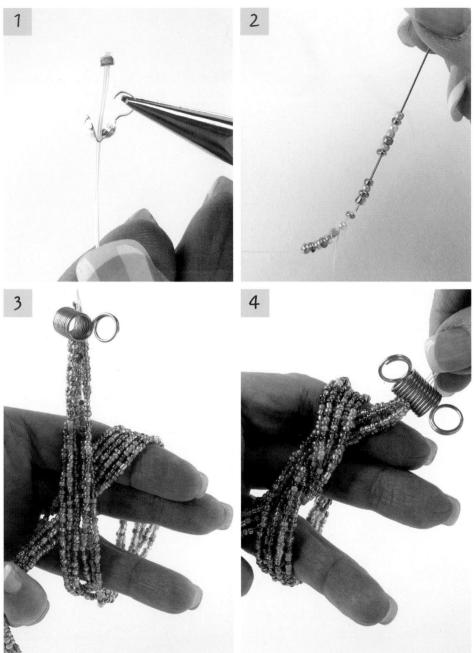

1 Cut Wildfire into three equal lengths, each about 65cm (25½in). Tie the three lengths together in an overhand knot (see page 36) about 2.5cm (1in) from one end and pull the knot tight. Seal the knot with clear nail varnish and allow to dry. Pass the short ends of all three strands of Wildfire through a crimp bead and slip the crimp bead over the knot. With chain-nose pliers, flatten the crimp bead (see page 12). Trim away any excess Wildfire from above the flattened crimp bead. Pass the three strands of Wildfire through a bead tip/calotte, going from the inside to the outside of the cup. Gently close the cup of the calotte over the flattened crimp.

2 Thread a split eye needle with approximately 3cm (1¼in) of one strand of the threads. Fill 45cm (17¾in) of thread with the assortment of green and silver seed beads. Remove the needle and use a bead stopper to keep the beads from coming off (see page 37). Repeat with the other two strands of Wildfire.
  Repeat steps 1 and 2 to form the other end of the necklace.

3 Holding both sides of the necklace together, place all six strands of seed beads into one bead stopper. Tie an overhand knot (see page 36) approximately 35cm (13¾in) from the calotte end.

4 Gently pull individual strands to remove any slack. There should be approximately 5cm (2in) of seed beads extending below the knot.

5 Remove a single strand from the bead stopper, then thread a split eye needle with approximately 3cm (1¼in) of the single strand of thread extending below the knot. Fill the strand with more seed beads. Add interest and texture by including two or three larger beads (choose from 6/0 silver seed beads, small and large green bicones or small and large AB crystal bicones) interspersed between the seed beads. Finish about 12cm (4¾in) below the knot.

6 Pass the needle through a crimp bead, then a green crystal bicone bead, and then a 6/0 silver seed bead (from the seed bead assortment).

7 Skipping the 6/0 silver seed bead, pass the needle back through the green crystal bicone bead. Continue to pass the needle and thread through the crimp bead and 2–3cm (¾–1¼in) of seed beads. With chain-nose pliers, flatten the crimp bead and trim any excess thread with flush cutters.

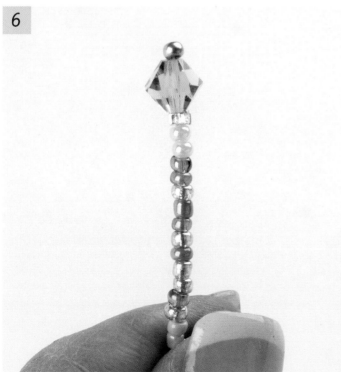

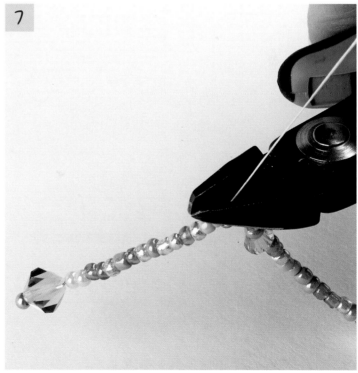

8 Repeat step 7 with the remaining thread strands. Stagger the larger beads that are placed between the seed beads so that they are more randomly placed and not side-by-side when all the strands are hanging together.

9 With round-nose pliers, close the hook above the calotte on one side of the necklace to form a loop.

10 Use chain-nose pliers to open a small jump ring (see 'Opening and Closing a Jump Ring' on page 14). Slip one side of the clasp onto the jump ring, attach the ring to the calotte loop at one end of the necklace and close the jump ring. Repeat steps 9 and 10 at the other end of the necklace.

Design inspiration

In this lush profusion of purple, copper and blue seed beads we have introduced a random mixture of beads in different shapes and sizes to give texture and interest. Fourteen strands of Wildfire have been passed through a larger bead to create the tassel effect.

BEADING AND BEYOND

In this chapter we take bead stringing to the next level.

We learn to float beads on tiger tail to create a soft, delicate appearance of the beads drifting freely around the neck.

We create asymetrical necklaces in eye-catching variations with gorgeous focal beads and variations of bead strands.

We dangle stunning crystals to strands of beads, to turn a classic necklace into an exquisite heirloom.

We form a bow tie from beads, to create a unique fashion accessory.

In this chapter, I want to show you some fun and easy ways in which to use the techniques from previous chapters, along with designer inspiration and helpful tips, to create unique and beautiful jewellery.

TOOLS

Chain-nose pliers

Flush cutters

Round-nose pliers

Bent-nose pliers

FLOATING PEARLS NECKLACE

Floating pearls in deep purple with a hint of green and blue reflect the ocean depths from which they come to create an illusion necklace, which is stunning in its simplicity.

What you learn

✎ How to float beads on beading wire using crimp beads

MATERIALS

9 12–15mm purple freshwater coin pearls
16 4mm purple freshwater round pearls
8 6mm silver-coloured diamante rondelle spacers
1m (39¼in) silver-coloured seven-strand beading wire/tiger tail
2 silver-coloured wire guardians
34 2mm silver-coloured crimp beads
2 6mm silver-coloured jump rings
1 silver-coloured clasp

1 Thread about 3cm (1¼in) of one end of the beading wire/tiger tail through a crimp bead and around a wire guardian. Pass the short end of the beading wire/tiger tail back through the crimp bead. Pull the wire tight with the crimp bead across the base of the wire guardian. With chain-nose pliers, flatten the crimp bead (see page 12). Thread the beading wire through one coin pearl and a crimp bead. Push the pearl up flush with the last crimp bead, ensuring that the short tail of wire is tucked into the pearl and hidden.

2 Push the lower crimp bead up flush with the pearl, and flatten with chain-nose pliers to hold it in place.

3 Thread the beading wire through a crimp bead, a small round pearl, a diamante spacer, a second small round pearl and a second crimp bead. Flatten the first crimp bead about 15mm (½in) down from the flattened crimp bead holding the coin pearl in place.

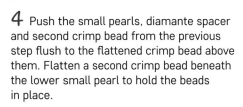

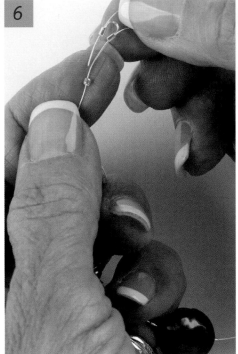

4 Push the small pearls, diamante spacer and second crimp bead from the previous step flush to the flattened crimp bead above them. Flatten a second crimp bead beneath the lower small pearl to hold the beads in place.

5 Thread the beading wire through another crimp bead, a second coin pearl and another crimp bead. Flatten the crimp bead above the coin pearl about 15mm (½in) from the flattened crimp bead that is below the small pearls and diamante spacer. Push the coin pearl and second crimp bead up flush with the flattened crimp bead above it, and flatten the lower crimp bead to hold the beads in place. Repeat steps 3 to 4 three more times until you reach the centre of the necklace, then continue the same sequence up the other side of the necklace, always checking to see that the pearls line up to create a mirror image on the second side.

6 To finish off the necklace, thread on a crimp bead, a coin pearl, a second crimp bead and pass it around a wire guardian. Flatten the crimp bead closest to the wire guardian so that the last coin pearl you thread on will rest side by side with the coin pearl on the opposite end of the necklace when the necklace is worn.

7 Thread the beading wire back through the last crimp bead and coin pearl. Pull out any excess wire to eliminate gaps. Flatten the crimp bead below the last coin pearl, and trim the excess beading wire with flush cutters.

8 Use chain-nose pliers to open a small jump ring (see 'Opening and Closing a Jump Ring' on page 14). Slip one side of the clasp onto the jump ring and attach to one end of the necklace and close. Repeat at the other end of the necklace.

Tips

- When floating beads, try to keep crimps tight against the beads they are holding in place unless you want them to move between crimps, which is another style in itself.

- You can also use a crimp tool to form a flattened crimp into a folded bead.

Design inspiration

Precious daisy beads are surrounded and
embellished by multiple strands of green and
yellow beads in varying shades, sizes and shapes.
This creates a stunning collar of floating beads.

PURPLE PASSION NECKLACE

A trio of faceted rainbow crystal hearts are the focus of this glamorous asymmetrical necklace. The richness of the mauve freshwater pearls is enhanced by the faceted sparkle of amethyst crystal rondelles to create a vision of tone on tone beauty.

What you learn

✎ How to make a basic loop
✎ How to create and balance an asymmetrical necklace

MATERIALS

3 22mm purple faceted crystal hearts
100–110 7–8mm mauve freshwater pearls
100–110 6 x 4mm amethyst faceted crystal rondelles
3 silver-coloured eye pins
6 2mm round silver metal beads
6 3mm round silver metal beads
1m (39½in) silver-coloured seven-strand beading wire/tiger tail
3 silver-coloured wire guardians
6 2mm silver-coloured crimp beads
1 22mm silver-coloured heart-shaped lobster/trigger clasp
2 9mm silver-coloured jump rings

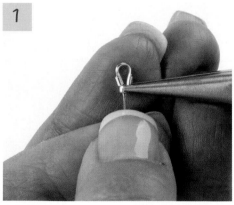

1 Thread about 3cm (1¼in) of one end of the beading wire/tiger tail through a crimp bead and around a wire guardian. Pass the short end of the beading wire/tiger tail back through the crimp bead. Pull the wire tight with the crimp bead across the base of the wire guardian. With chain-nose pliers, flatten the crimp bead (see page 12).

2 Thread approximately 78 pearls onto beading wire with a 3mm silver metal bead at each end.

3 Pass the beading wire/tiger tail through a crimp bead, leaving a loop. Then pass the beading wire/tiger tail back through the crimp bead and the next two beads. Pull the wire tight to eliminate any gaps or exposed wire. With chain-nose pliers, flatten the crimp bead across the base of the wire guardian. Trim away any excess beading wire using flush cutters.

4 Repeat steps 1 to 3 to string approximately 104 amethyst crystal rondelles with a silver metal bead at each end onto another strand of beading wire/tiger tail.

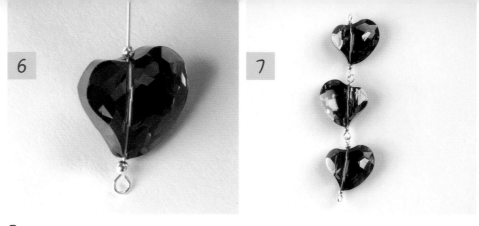

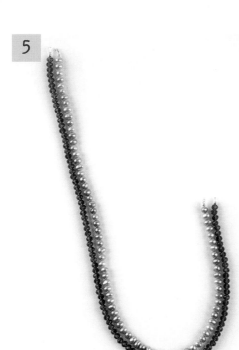

5 Check that the crystal strand is slightly longer than the pearl strand so that when placed together, the crystals hang just below the pearls.

Make a second strand of pearls using steps 1–2 with approximately 29 pearls and a 3mm silver metal bead at each end; attach a wire guardian to one end only.

6 Thread a small metal bead, a crystal heart and a second metal bead onto an eye pin. Make a basic loop with the wire at the top of the heart, following the instructions below, Make basic loops for the other two crystal hearts in the same way.

7 Join the three hearts together by opening the loop at the bottom of one heart and slipping it through the loop at the top of a second heart and closing the loop with pliers.

MAKING A BASIC LOOP

1 With chain-nose pliers, bend the wire extending above the bead at right-angles, as close to the bead as possible.

2 Cut off excess wire, leaving a small arm of about 1cm (³/₈in).

3 With round-nose pliers, grab the very end of the pin about 6mm (¼in) from the tip of the pliers. Twist the wire back towards where the wire comes out of the bead, wrapping it tightly around a barrel of the pliers to make a loop. The finished loop should be positioned centrally over the hole of the bead.

8

9

10

8 Open the top loop of the first heart and slip it around the tiger-tail loop at one end of the short strand of pearls. Close the loop.

9 Open the bottom loop of the bottom heart and slip it around the tiger-tail loops at one end of both the long strand of pearls and the strand of crystal rondelles

10 Use chain-nose pliers to open a large jump ring (see page 14). Slip the heart-shaped lobster/trigger clasp onto the jump ring and attach to the loose ends of both the long pearl strand and the crystal strand and close. Open an 8mm jump ring and attach it to the open end of the short strand of pearls at the other end of the necklace.

Design inspiration

Three strands of small coco beads offset and balance the single strand of gorgeous polished bayong beads. They are divided by a large coconut shell bead.

CRYSTAL DANGLES NECKLACE

Lush creamy pearls mixed with sparkling Aurora Borealis crystals create an exquisite necklace of understated perfection.

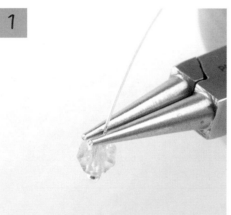

1 Start by making the 'dangles'. Onto a ball-end headpin, thread the 12mm crystal bead. Following the instructions on page 29, make a wrapped loop. Repeat with the four other crystals and the two oval freshwater pearls and four small round freshwater pearls. Set aside until step 3.

2 Following the instructions on page 12, thread about 3cm (1¼in) of one end of the beading wire/tiger tail through a crimp bead and around a wire guardian. Pass the short end of the beading wire/tiger tail back through the crimp bead. Pull the wire tight with the crimp bead across the base of the wire guardian. With chain-nose pliers, flatten the crimp bead.

Tip

• Sometimes the holes in freshwater pearls can be very small and therefore difficult to pass tiger tail or beading wire through twice at step 4. If this should be the case, use a pearl reamer to enlarge the hole.

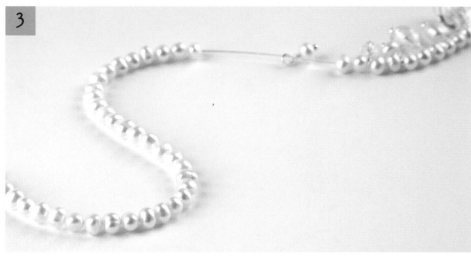

3 String onto the beading wire 35 small freshwater pearls followed by the dangles in the following sequence (the dangles are separated by small pearls):
- small pearl dangle
- two small pearls
- small crystal dangle
- two small pearls
- small pearl dangle
- two small pearls
- medium crystal dangle
- two small pearls
- oval pearl dangle
- two small pearls
- large crystal dangle
- two small pearls
- oval pearl dangle
- two small pearls
- medium crystal dangle
- two small pearls
- small pearl dangle
- two small pearls
- small crystal dangle
- two small pearls
- small pearl dangle

4 Pass the beading wire/tiger tail through a crimp bead and around a wire guardian (see page 12 for guidance). Pass the beading wire/tiger tail back through the crimp bead and the next two beads. Pull the wire tight to eliminate any gaps or exposed wire. With chain-nose pliers, flatten the crimp bead across the base of the wire guardian. Trim away any excess beading wire using flush cutters.

5 Use chain-nose pliers to open a small jump ring (see 'Opening and Closing a Jump Ring' on page 14). Slip one side of the clasp onto the jump ring and attach to one end of the necklace and close with the pliers. Repeat to attach the other side of the clasp to the other side of the necklace.

Design inspiration

The soft delicate hues of pale green fluorite form the base of this necklace with dangling faceted clear crystals and amethyst. Fluorite, a lovely semi-precious stone, is said to boost the immune system as well as increasing concentration.

BOW TIE NECKLACE

• •

The versatility of beading wire makes it easy to form this special-feature bow from beads. The combination of crystal bicones and crystal rondelles adds texture and interest to the repeated design of this elegant bow tie necklace.

What you learn

✎ How to create a beaded bow

MATERIALS

116 4mm red crystal bicones
58 6 x 4mm jet faceted crystal rondelles
58 4 x 3mm silver metallic crystal rondelles
3 8 x 6mm silver metallic crystal rondelles
152 10/0 satin silver seed beads
3 4cm (1½in) silver-coloured head pins
1.5m (59in) silver-coloured seven-strand beading wire/tiger tail
4 silver-coloured wire guardians
6 2mm silver-coloured crimp beads
2 6mm silver-coloured jump rings
1 9mm silver-coloured jump ring
1 silver-coloured lobster/trigger clasp

1

2

1 Following the instructions on page 12, thread about 3cm (1¼in) of one end of the beading wire/tiger tail through a crimp bead and around a wire guardian. Pass the short end of the beading wire/tiger tail back through the crimp bead. Pull the wire tight with the crimp bead across the base of the wire guardian. With chain-nose pliers, flatten the crimp bead.

2 String the following sequence of beads three times (this will be one tail of the bow):
• silver seed bead
• red bicone bead
• 4 x 6mm jet rondelle bead
• red bicone bead
• silver seed bead
• 3 x 4mm silver rondelle bead

Finish this tail by adding to the beading wire:
• silver seed bead
• red bicone bead
• 4 x 6mm jet rondelle bead
• red bicone bead
• silver seed bead

3

3 Add to the beading wire a 6 x 8mm silver rondelle (this bead will form the centre of the bow).

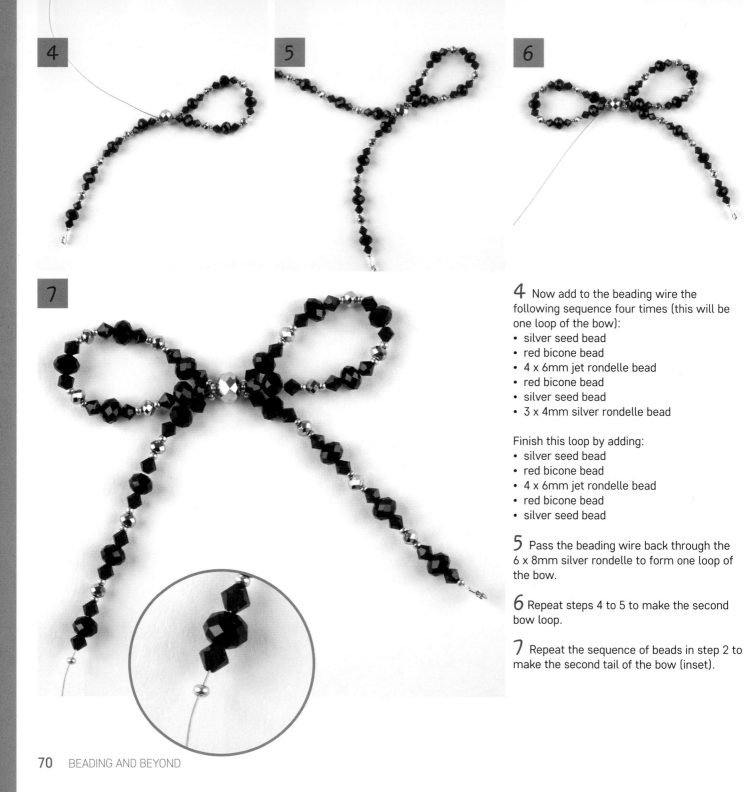

4 Now add to the beading wire the following sequence four times (this will be one loop of the bow):
- silver seed bead
- red bicone bead
- 4 x 6mm jet rondelle bead
- red bicone bead
- silver seed bead
- 3 x 4mm silver rondelle bead

Finish this loop by adding:
- silver seed bead
- red bicone bead
- 4 x 6mm jet rondelle bead
- red bicone bead
- silver seed bead

5 Pass the beading wire back through the 6 x 8mm silver rondelle to form one loop of the bow.

6 Repeat steps 4 to 5 to make the second bow loop.

7 Repeat the sequence of beads in step 2 to make the second tail of the bow (inset).

8 Pick up a crimp bead onto wire, then pass it around a wire guardian and back through the crimp bead and three beads. Pull out the excess wire, flatten the crimp bead with chain-nose pliers and cut any excess wire using flush cutters.

9 Take a 50cm (19¾in) strand of beading wire and make a fold approximately 3cm (1¼in) from one end. Place the fold around the beading wire of one bow loop between the fourth red bicone and silver seed bead from the central large silver rondelle on the top of one bow loop (see inset). Pass both ends of the wire through a crimp bead and with chain-nose pliers flatten the crimp as close as possible so it slips in between the bicone and seed bead.

10 String the following sequence of beads onto the beading wire leading off the loop:
- silver seed bead
- red bicone bead
- 4 x 6mm jet rondelle bead
- red bicone bead
- silver seed bead
- 3 x 4mm silver rondelle bead

Repeat this sequence 18 times, then finish the sequence by adding to the beading wire:
- silver seed bead
- red bicone bead
- 4x6mm jet rondelle bead
- red bicone bead

Add a crimp bead at the end of the length of beading wire, then pass the wire around a wire guardian. Thread the wire back through the crimp bead and two or three beads. Pull out the excess wire, flatten the crimp bead with chain-nose pliers, and cut the excess wire with flush cutters. Repeat this step to make the other side of the necklace leading up from the loop.

11 Use chain-nose pliers to open a large jump ring (see 'Opening and Closing a Jump Ring' on page 14). Slip the lobster/trigger clasp onto the jump ring and attach it to one of the loose ends of the necklace.

12 Open an 8mm jump ring and attach it to the other loose end of the necklace.

13 To make the dangles for the ends of the bow tails, thread a 6 x 8mm silver rondelle onto a ball-end headpin. Make a basic loop (see page 62) and attach the dangle to the wire guardian on one of the bow tails. Repeat for the other bow tail to complete the piece.

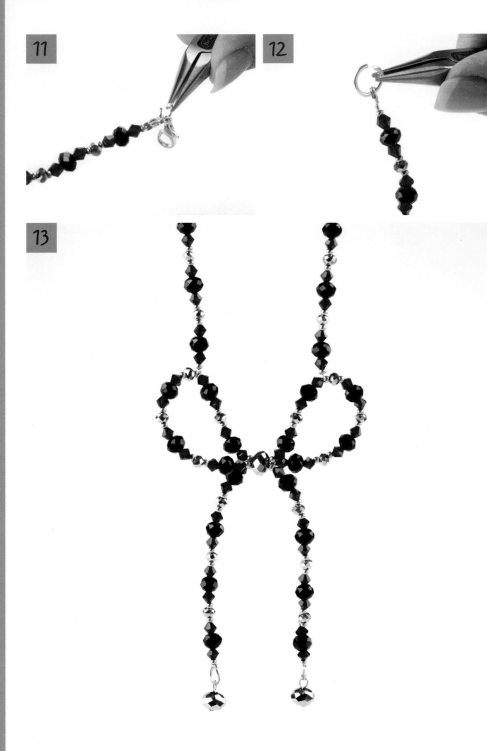

Design inspiration

The gorgeous opalescent and transparent aqua beads with silver accents give a fresh alternative to our Bow Tie necklace. Why not add more 'wow' to your bow by doubling it? A double bow is easy enough to make with two bows based around the same central bead.

Is there a special little person you know who would love to have a Bow Tie necklace of their own? We have used smaller beads to make a miniature version that will make you a real hit with a young friend or relation!

Jewellery Jargon Buster

AB (AURORA BOREALIS)

A steam treatment for beads that creates a shimmering effect in rainbow colours.

BEADING WIRE/TIGER TAIL

Multiple strands of fine stainless steel wire, tightly twisted together and covered with a nylon coating. Used for stringing and/or floating beads and findings to create durable and flexible pieces.

BALL-END HEADPINS

A headpin is a length of wire with a decorative round ball end, which holds a bead on the wire while a loop is formed above it, to attach the bead to a jewellery piece.

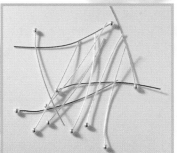

BICONE BEADS

Glass beads shaped like two faceted cones joined together at their base.

CALOTTES

see Bead tips or calottes

BEAD CAPS

These are usually made of metal. They are used to enhance a bead or stone, to go between the end of a string of beads and the clasp, to protect precious beads from rubbing against each other or to hide discolouration or blemishes on beads.

CHARMS

Decorative pendants, trinkets or beads that may signify something important to the wearer. Used to decorate jewellery including earrings, bracelets and necklaces.

BEAD TIPS/CALOTTES

These are small metal findings that resemble clam shells with hooks at the ends. The cup closes over a knot and/or a crimp bead to conceal and protect the end while giving a professional finish. The hook is used to attach the clasp when finishing a jewellery piece.

CLASPS

Devices or fasteners used for attaching or holding the ends of jewellery together.

A lobster clasp is in the shape of a lobster claw. It is held closed by a spring that is operated by a small lever. Also called a parrot clasp or a trigger clasp.

A toggle clasp is made up of a bar and a ring with the bar fitting through the ring to fasten the clasp. The beads next to the bar must be small enough to pull through the ring (or a few jump rings or links of chain can be added to the bar end).

CRIMP BEADS

Small beads made of soft metal that hold components in place when flattened with pliers. Used to secure wire ends when attaching clasps or beads to beading wire. Also used to float beads on wire or certain chains.

CRYSTAL RONDELLES

Faceted crystal beads that have a 'squashed' rounded shape. Also known as faceted crystal rondelles, faceted crystal doughnuts and squashed round crystals.

DIAMANTE RONDELLE SPACERS

Also called crystal rondelle spacers. These look like tyre hubcaps with diamante stones decorating the rim. They are used between beads to add interest and sparkle.

EYE PINS

Lengths of wire with a pre-formed loop end used to link two things together.

FACETED CRYSTAL RONDELLES

see Crystal rondelles

FRESHWATER PEARLS

These are produced in freshwater mussels which create a pearl sac to seal off an irritant, usually introduced by human intervention.

GLASS PEARLS

These are made to imitate pearls, with a glass base that is then dipped in a coating to create colour and lustre.

GLITTER BALLS

Clay beads with crystal pavé – an all-over sparkling surface. There are different grades depending on the quality of the crystals, with Czech crystals at the high end and acrylic 'glass' at the opposite end.

HEADPINS

Lengths of wire that can be ball-end (see right), flat or decorative (right, bottom). Flat headpins have a flat head like a nail. The end holds a bead on the wire while a loop is formed at the other end and used to attach beads to a jewellery piece.

JUMP RINGS

Circles of wire, available in varying thicknesses with a join allowing the ring to be opened and closed. Used to attach two components. Available in different shapes with round and oval being the most popular.

METAL SPACER BEADS

Beads made of plated precious or base metal. They come in many different shapes and sizes and are used to separate patterns on beaded jewellery.

SEED BEADS

Small beads made from long pipes of glass, often used for weaving jewellery designs, for stringing or as spacer beads. The most popular sizes start at 15/0, which is the smallest, up to 6/0, which are called pony beads.

TASSELS

A decorative feature that was traditionally made of bunched loose threads. Tassels can now be made from all sorts of different materials including beads, chain, fabric, etc.

WILDFIRE BEADING THREAD

This thermally-bonded braided thread is strong, durable and waterproof, and is particularly popular for stringing and weaving beads.

WIRE

Craft wire comes in a number of different gauges (diameter) and colours. The higher the gauge, the thinner the wire.

WIRE GUARDIANS

Horseshoe-shaped metal tubes that are open at the curve and used to protect wires and threads in places where they get more wear and tear. They give a professional look to jewellery endings.

WOOD BEADS

All sorts of types of wood are used to make beads in different shapes and colours which can be natural or dyed. They are usually light-weight and, in their natural state, give an organic feel to jewellery pieces.

Tools

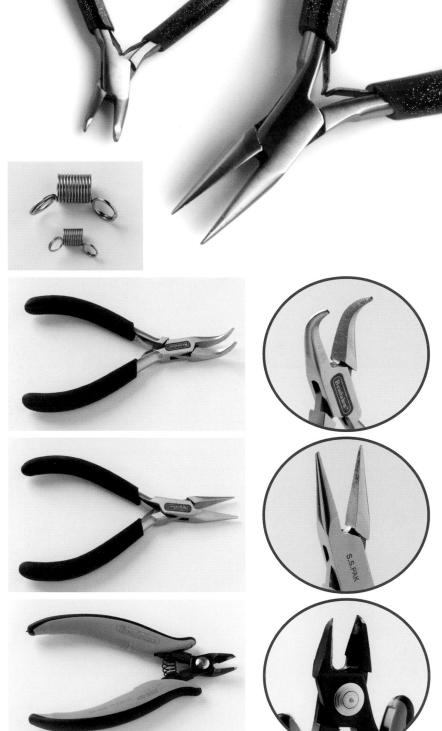

BEAD STOPPER

A gadget made up of tightly coiled metal wire that is used to secure the end of a project in progress, keeping beads, wire or components in position.

BENT-NOSE PLIERS

Similar to chain-nose pliers but with curved jaws. Half the length of the jaws is bent at an angle away from the centre of the pliers. These are used to reach into tight places, bend wire, open and close jump rings, close bead tips/calottes and attach clasps. The bent jaws allow access without blocking vision.

CHAIN-NOSE PLIERS

These have jaws that are flat on the inside and rounded on the outside. They are used to hold findings, components, wire, cords, etc. They are good for getting into tight spaces where fingers can't reach and can hold components more securely than fingers. When working with wire, make sure the insides of the jaws are smooth, as ridged or textured jaws will mark the wire.

FLUSH CUTTERS

The jaws of flush cutters have a flat side and a bevelled side. They are used to make smooth, flat, neat cuts in wire. The flat side gives a straight cut and the bevelled side gives a V-shaped cut.

REAMER AND BRADAWL

A round, tapered file used to clear, smooth or enlarge the inside of the bead hole; a reamer is also useful when tying knots. The one shown on the left is battery operated.

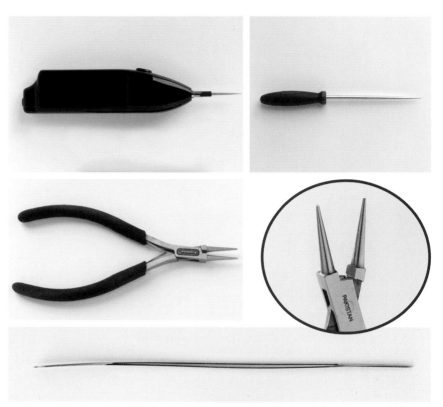

ROUND-NOSE PLIERS

Both jaws are tapered cones used for creating loops as well as bending and shaping wire. Having tapered cones for barrels allows different sizes of loop to be formed according to what is required. Most commonly used to create loops on eye pins or headpins that are used for attaching beads and components.

SPLIT EYE NEEDLE

This has an eye that spans almost the whole length of the needle and makes it easy to thread most sizes of thread and cord. It is incredibly flexible and perfect for bead projects.

Index